Stretching the Window

Poems by T.M. Göttl

A Buffalo ZEF Publication

STRETCHING THE WINDOW

All Poems Copyright ©2007 T.M. Göttl

All rights reserved. No part of this book may be reproduced in any form or by any means without written permission from the author, except in the case of brief quotations embodied in critical articles or reviews. Unauthorized reproduction may result in a plague of squirrels sent to nibble off your toes.

"Fairway of the Bears" was previously published in *The Mill*.
"Searching for the Big Skies" won second place in the 2007 Wayne College Regional Writing Awards.
"Time" was performed and recorded for The Poet's Haven.

Cover photo by Gary Fossaceca.

Cover art and design by Korrin Bonnigson.

Author's photo by Korrin Bonnigson.

Edited by Korrin Bonnigson and Zach Freidhof.

Published by Buffalo ZEF   www.buffalozef.net

ISBN: 978-1-59916-470-0

*for my Göttl Opa and my Kun Opa,
who I know are still watching out for me.*

ACKNOWLEDGMENTS

Deepest appreciation to the following:

My beautiful colleagues at Buffalo ZEF, for your art, advice, hands, hugs, and long (and sometimes unproductive) nights. Zach and Korrin, this book is yours, from inspiration to publication.

My family and especially my parents, for love and support, even during those times when I was most difficult to love and support. John and Bev Hutchens, for hosting the first poetry night I ever attended, and for being my "poetry family" ever since. April Brooks, for taking me to that first poetry night.

The Erewhon Poets and everyone at Erewhon Gallery. Mark Kuhar and all the deep cleveland poets. Sharon Kubasak, Michael Dolzani, and everyone in the Baldwin-Wallace English Department. Wayne College and the Poetry, Prose, and Acoustical Jam. Patricia Nemitz, for planting the music in my soul. UPS Supply Chain Solutions. The number 52. Marcus Bales. David Ullman. Brunswick Art Works, and Jim and Eileen Smalley at Insights. Scott Fetterolf, may your soul find rest in God's peace. Iceland. Peter Hessman. Ursula and Apollonova. My "sisters," for so many inspiring conversations that have worked their way into these poems. All things zesty, fifty-four cents, the last piece of pizza, and pears. The Kid with the Hair in His Face. The Poet's Haven. I-71, I-65, and I-77. Everyone from Canton's First Friday Poetry Competitions. Anyone who ever offered me time behind the microphone. All the friends, old and new, who came to a reading, gave an opinion or a hug, or have just been there for me. Czeslaw Milosz, Ayn Rand, Jack London, Dostoevsky, Tchaikovsky, and U2, for inspiration.

And to God, for sending His angels to whisper their songs, that I might write them down.

To everyone who picks up this book, I wish you life, love, and light!

CONTENTS

Muse 3
Confessions 5
Da Vinci Helicopter 7
Disillusion 9
Upon Waking 12
Kismet is a Town in Kansas 13
Fable of Relocation 15
Pavilions 17
The Ball 19
Crab Walking with the Sand Gnomes 21
From Music City 23
Fairway of the Bears 25
Time 27
Christmas Morning 30
Early May in Ohio 32
The Lazarus Dance 35
Argument in the Chapel 37
Searching for the Big Skies 40
At the Grocery Store 42
Just Another Wednesday 43
The Nomads 45
Terrestrial Nostalgia 47
Across the River 49
Indigo Freight Train 51
Through My Orange Window 53

Throwing Rocks	55
Almonds	57
Lament and Chronicle	59
Paranoia	61
Rain	63
The Rabbits of St. Joseph	65
Run, Run 'til You're Far Away	68
Between	70
Story	71
Tripping Over Giants	73
On the Day of Broken Bells	75
Uncertainty	77
Reluctant Hallelujah	79
Exit	81
Deus Ex Machina	83
The Night Children	85
A Pedestrian Unexpected	87
3 a.m. at Hotel Kazakhstan	89
Saving Souls	92
The Babies of the Stone Wings: The Final Song of Milo	94
Note from the Anonymous Lover	98
Locking Windows, Lifting Ceilings	100
Sailor	103
Escape Tones	104
Detour	106
Lost	108
Out of the Desert	110

Stretching the Window

MUSE

Have you ever seen a man
working the job God built for him?
You'll know him
by his feathers,
white and gold.
They sprout from his fingers
and toes
so he can fly to the moon.

And this moonbird perches
on the corner of that silver smile
to sing his sweet cock-a-doodle
until the stars buzz down
like enlightening bugs,
sitting in the jars of his eyes.

The moonbird sings
in the key of fire and lace,
raking the green from grass
to scatter across the dancing
coyotes and skunks
and crickets,
in this secretly glory-eerie
ballet for midnight love.

You will know
the song of the moonbird
when your heart clacks
under railroad ties,
a bump and jostle
for every minute lost
to curled-up safety,
to closed eyes, and to fear
of stretching your thoughts
over the trees
because you just might find
a truth grinning back.

CONFESSIONS

At age five, I aspired
to grow up and become
an animal:
a dog or cat or bird,
or some such thing, depending
on recent Discovery Channel specials
featuring wombats or lemurs or
hedgehogs. I cut out cardboard tails
and ears, or draped grandma's afghan
around my arms for wings.

But, one cannot
be a lemur while wearing a jumper. Boys
must not wear skirts, and so
I grew up a tomboy instead
of a muskrat, shunning
lace and bows, petticoats and
pinafores. (In fact,
I don't even know
what a pinafore is.) The closest
I've come to girlishness
was play-acting at diva for
proms or dear friends' weddings,
or other affairs requiring
a small tonnage of frills.

I've worn makeup exactly
three times, and nail polish only
for the beautiful joy that
the mess of paint brings.
My flat and wide feet prefer
cork-soled sandals, rejecting all
heel-height whatsoever.
I still refuse skirts
under all but the most
extenuating circumstances.

"Someday," I tell myself, "I
will buy a crinkly, flouncy skirt,
gathered here and
trailing there, like the cutest,
most attractive of curtains."
But today, the
dressing room reminds me
that mine is not
a window frame for
hanging "cute" curtains.

DA VINCI HELICOPTER

Standing on a desert hill,
learning songs from the pebbled lizards,
I could see four people
running single file, running in long gray coats,
running to the shore.
They shouted in galloping Scottish accents,
and threw diamonds—chains and pendants and
bracelets and giant rings—threw it all
along with lines from epic mythology
into the lake.

Somewhere, maybe in a bishop's basement,
heavy smoke dampens a stormy piano,
the black and white and gray notes blurring together
in a thunderhead hanging above
a conclave of Bohemians,
sailboats cut adrift and blown from shore.
They plan with restricted voices
beneath the fumes of foreign whiskey and
witch-doctored tea, busting apart the physics
of every rhyme that Goethe wrote,
and kicking open boxes of dragonflies
to mingle with the ladybugs and grasshoppers
in the air. Until they realize
there are no insects there, only

Da Vinci helicopters, and it doesn't matter
if they've been carved from
stone or ink or sand. Flightless birds
borrow the black feathers
shed from angel wings,
and they fumble with tiny metal harps or
tin flutes, because hesitation
stole their voices.
Between all the viruses and
landslides, the tabloid witnesses and
ruptured trust,
I need to wonder
if even the grizzlies still exist
outside the knocking bass and fog of some
western dreamer's night.

DISILLUSION

I'm worn from chasing after
evaporating rainbows, and
unicorns charging with
papier-mâché horns,
and faeries whose wings
have been plucked.
The heroes here all wear
moth-eaten capes,
and the prophets,
sharing their blessed tongues,
wake up next to bloodied swords
between their sheets.
If I drop the silver weights
from my ears,
the trees have promised me
a perfect, round, white city.
But it doesn't matter.
The saints don't listen,
even after offerings of
automated mansions and gold-plated automobiles
and seventeen weeks of
fasting beneath a full moon;
they never foreclose on our debts.
I know that doves never cry at night,
nor do they linger near the

dinner plates of emperors.
And even the false gods,
those gluttonous concrete monuments,
live in smoke-damaged temples,
guarded by priests
who paint lies across their eyes.
Treaties were signed,
under ringing bells and bonfire light,
but the scars of old footprints
were never repaved
under streets of crystal glass.
Thieves unlatched all the cages,
freeing many colored things
with feathers and fur
and bright golden eyes.
And come morning,
they handed the cages back,
filled, instead, with small devils
who chase us out the windows
and off of rooftops,
falling up and falling down
and even falling sideways, just
to see what it feels like
to either fly or collide.
So again I ask, with black ribbons tied
around my wrists, while the brokers
chop my feet from my ankles, please
send tomorrow, just one

tomorrow.
Because the rivers never know
if they are leaving
or returning home again.

UPON WAKING

Screech owls
etching
hieroglyphics
with their talons
into papyrus
and plaster
walls.

Blue fear
shivers,
landing
tentatively,
against bold oceans,
biting the tips
off protective fingers.

Independent pelts,
lacquered
with spots
and stripes,
lead
the malignantly
violent
through submissive waves
and coldness.

KISMET IS A TOWN IN KANSAS

The prophet blessed and dissolved
my hate, transmutated it,
into a murky, watery melancholy.
And I left to live
with the lonely race of snowboarders,
superheroes, and astronauts.
Not that I am brave, like them;
I am a coward.
But somehow, my weight grew
rejected by the earth,
so I joined those
wingéd and lonely pilgrims,
washing the western sunsets
from their feet.
They have no
soulmates, followers, partners,
past or future,
and they pray to every
deity, god, and nymph
for survival against one more moment
of terrifying joy.

With no footholds or armrests,
cultural memory draws from ancients,
remembering demons, elves, and monsters.

Our race of flyers believes
as the Icelanders, who
build doors into boulders for elf-houses,
and daily, scramble Adam and Eve
with faerie theology. God still walks
at the top of the world among the Icelanders.
But we? We have no choice but
blind and blinding faith, or else the gods
tear their weather from beneath us,
and we fall.

FABLE OF RELOCATION

Tell me, didn't you want this noise?
And the gravel, and the cigarette
ashes in the street?
And your bare feet running
from those old, icy roads, that wrapped
around a century
of falling plaster
and burning books?

But now, you're shocked
at rock stars, with open arms,
waiting for angels to fall?

You're still just a country girl,
banking your dust against hot steel;
still just a city girl,
stumbling through the corn. So
take these pigeons from your inkwells,
and pray that you'll start finding
truth in lies. Just like
the curled, Byzantine spires,
blooming over naked,
aluminum shields and
asphalt-broken stairwells.

Can you see
to pull the thorn from the lion's paw?
Or would you rather just hide
all your seaside roses,
sealed inside black mason jars,
without numbers, or labels,
or sunlit bouquets?

PAVILIONS

Signed on with a flock of snowbirds,
we all flew south, into the sun,
risking melted wings and swollen, Icarus tears,
for a chance at swallowing
the songs of the mulberry moth,
falling from the equator.

Skimming the peaks of a blue pavilion colony,
we checked inside each tent,
finding tiny brick walls
in all except one:
holding a small pink moon,
translucent, dusty,
tied in yellowed newsprint.

It was cracked,

and leaking a sweet, sticky gold,
because inside dwelt a tiny thing,
an owl or panther cub, untested
wings and eyes, unused
to light and air,
and prematurely covered
with a full white fur.

Ululations of separation, its voice
tore the darkness from behind the stars,
leaving constellations hanging cold against the naked night,
and wise men, paralyzed,
in their satins and velvets.

Slamming car doors, pitted gravel,
metal singeing metal: the leavings
of evaporated storybooks, pooled
like molten silver on the berm.

In waist-high grass and Queen Anne's lace,
the twilit monarchs opened and closed
one thousand orange windows,
while we groped for sleep
in the blinded corners
and the crowded foyers.

THE BALL

With my easel strapped to my back
and my disinterested eyes widened with
new-age nightmares, I walked past
the glass-walled ballroom,
when a gargoyle herded me through the doors.
Pepper thickened the air, while the dinner guests
bullied me from corner to corner
—into French chefs and cowboys,
at least one Viking princess, and other
monsters who stalk the misguided and lost,
trapped between the walls of
airports and subway stations.
I clung to a grandfather clock,
hoping to avoid reentering
the hurricaning crowd,
but the man inside,
wearing gray pin-stripes and a black bowler,
banged against his window,
laughing and refusing
to perform any magic.
A leather-armored Roman and a steel-clad knight,
pried me from the clock, dragged me
to the front of the room, and dropped me
before a dark queen. She
sat on a throne of raptor talons and
water lilies that growled and bloomed like

tiny lions, while a mahogany spire
rose above each shoulder, topped
with a white and indifferent owl.
Two feathered lizards, the
twin half-breeds of eagles and chameleons,
nipped at my approach,
before intertwining in battle or love—which
was indistinguishable. The queen,
wrapped all in gold and blood,
declared, with a white and pointed finger,
her intolerance for scruffy free-radicals
who crack shockwaves into
rainy days and break listlessness
into bold black marks,
who peek under the darkness at eclipses
in search of anthemic love.

I stood, dusted my knees, and smiling,
stated that, yes,
I too dance in the garage,
and dance in my kitchen, and
dance to the hold music on the telephone.
I dance on my way to the copy machine,
and I dance with my cart down the cereal aisle.

And then I danced, with my easel on my back,
out the door and away from the queen
with her mongrel court of demigod vandals.

CRAB WALKING WITH THE SAND GNOMES

Sandals and flashlights
and dune grass and darkness:
children and their adults, both,
drop dabs of light, spilled and rolling,
bouncing from the dunes
to the glowing salt line,
where moonlight and waterbugs
fuel the tide pools that deconstruct
all of our yesterdays.
The time here has a habit
of evaporating,
like a camouflaged spook
twisted around the palm leaves or
stuck and hiding beneath the pier.

With their squinting windows,
the beach cabins watch
you and the other
distracted excursionists,
trailing red or yellow plastic buckets and
two-dollar, mossy fishing nets
through the dark.

A sound like a cello
rubs across the sky and pulls
your eyes east to a fishing boat,
whose rigging is snagged
between the water and the starshine,
calling out with a signal light,
hoping to sail home, skimming Slavic melodies.

Down the beach, you hear a
shuffling and a ten-year-old yelp:
one more ghost crab
trapped in a basket of flashlight beams.
No more building castles
or digging jewel-studded dungeons;
the sand gnomes have lost
one more tenant tonight.
And you just saunter through their city,
wondering what sandpiper princesses
might live at the top
of a seashell staircase.

FROM MUSIC CITY

A shaman once wore these pajamas
paired with a bird-faced mask,
feathers and flannel snowflakes
together,
used as transport to
secluded glowing attic rooms, or
mountain trails populated by cougars, or
silver alleys where amateurs practiced
dealing tarot cards and ballads.

This shaman lived
in the city built of music,
housed in one especially sturdy
and living song.
And now that I own his
extreme pajamas,
they climb glaciers and waterfalls,
snowboard through avalanches,
and skip across the river Styx,
just to return to their home.
They play poker, cutting deals
with herds of antelope and hyenas.
And flocks of geese at midnight
fly us all, alligators and
groundhogs alike,

to the northern,
purple seas.
We meet strange travelers,
people whose skins
change colors—first cobalt, now
vermillion—
and drop riddles from their mouths,
which scamper or buzz away,
inventing new species of
salamander and insect with every word.

And wearing these pajamas,
I seek out those between places,
inhabited mostly by children,
the ones who still remember paradise,
and haven't yet been cut
from the big humming of the planets.

FAIRWAY OF THE BEARS

On a Saturday night
I am watching polar bears on TV;
their yellowed bulk,
drugged and stuffed into nets,
flown to somewhere in Canada
dangling from a helicopter.
They gently spill onto the frozen ocean,
and a movie star turned naturalist
pets their groggy, bobbing heads
before they can fully wake
and eat him.

And I think:
I want to be a flying bear,
hung in a hammock from a giant mosquito,
louder than the swarms of people
with their screaming, whining, sticky cubs
who come to the zoo to stare at me
and my private swimming pool.

I could eat them all,
but I'm not quite awake,
not quite asleep,
but somewhere between the chilly wake-up bath
and the recurring dream about tea with the alligator.

Somewhere in the middle,
the fuzzy, blurry ground drops from my feet,
then rises back to kiss them.

And when I finally roll into the snow,
blinking in the fresh purple arctic light,
the poking fingers and the metal dragonfly
all melt away and seep into the ground.
And I have always been home.

TIME

Time, and the march
of army boots,
and metal chairs, and the
midnight howl of a panther train.

Time, and the sea lord
calling back the herds,
and the seventh breaking
of the hardwood stair.

Time, and a white coat,
cigarettes, and coffee.

Time, and the refrigerated
cellular automotive
facsimile liquid crystal
satellite malfunction.

Time, and the lack of confidence,
reflected in faded
cathedral glass.

Time, and aluminum eagle wings,
and the painted skydivers, and
the telescoping highways.

Time, and a minted peace
and a pinecone rustle,
and a chipmunk soul.

Time, because everyone's written
a poem about heartbreak
and an empty hotel room.

Time, and the concrete lions, and
telephone poles, and the copper, copper
saxophone strings.

Time, and the burning pages,
the empty bottles, the distorted
static music. Time, and the black keys,
white keys, gray keys, colored keys,
computer keys, car keys,
house keys, major keys,
minor keys.

Time, and the red ink, and the
black water.

Time through a glass,
around your neck,
under your feet, and
in your pocket.

Time, and a house without ceilings
a front lawn full of hands,
and a basement
full of feet
and folded prayers.

Time, and a red, paper kite,
hunting through the starshine.

CHRISTMAS MORNING

A gray chickadee tilts his
black furry cap against the sun,
and a wolf upsets the snow
settled in his mane
as I walk past them on the trail,
blinking the snow-blindness out of my eyes.
Each parishioner
will leave the church this morning,
carrying a heavy, iron bell, to ring
and remember
that God and Faith and Hope and Peace
used to be more than buzzwords
and red-blue propaganda.
Because a small black mouse of doubt
crawls into each of our minds,
gnawing away at wonder and magic
and how this story ends, whether
it's with broken wedding rings or…
I can't remember.
What if we forget
that each step and breath is miraculous? That
we only live now because some ancestors,
by chance or providence,
whether princesses or serfs,
outlasted plagues and inquisitions

and golden-eyed monsters?
What about the ones
who forget to exist?
Will they remember, on a morning
with sun curling around the snow,
as a balloon pilot waves
from his painted travels,
before wind and a tall hill
swallow him away?

EARLY MAY IN OHIO

Fishing rods and tackle boxes
dawdle home behind
three boys,
muddy at the ankles
and half-wearing,
half-dragging,
their winter jackets,
on which Mom insisted,
because early May in Ohio
means the air still tastes
like leftover flakes,
cold and stale.

They are eleven.

And pause a minute
answering a smiling lady,
lonely with age
and sweeping wet grass
from her driveway.
They eagerly wrap
smooth adult nonchalance
too tightly around
adolescent excitement,

and just might
explode colorful little
bits of modesty
all over the walk.

They are expected
at a monitor
blasting battle droids,
not roaming sidewalks,
drenched in sunshine
and pond water,
seeking a suburban
wilderness.

They speak
the secret language
of eleven-year-old boys,
of tender shoves
and boasting
big-armed gestures
and maybe an
experimental cuss
here and there,
coupled with an
unripened swagger
of cool,
modeled on dads and
teen-aged brothers.

Too big for them now,
they stumble and trip
on the baggy ends
of this man-love
sign language,
all the while
insisting and pleading
that it fits just right.

Slowly,
they will grow into
this adulthood,
bought too soon and young;
this shiny green freshness,
their desperate imitations,
will age to a rough
suit of bark,
just snug enough.
But not before today,
when they still drop gear
and knees
in the grass,
chasing a toad
through the yard,
and bringing home
blue jeans
stained with the spring.

THE LAZARUS DANCE

Lazarus spoke,
and ten-thousand iridescent starlings
flooded the sky, leaving
tiny blue triangles behind.
Nine maidens, wrapped in white gowns
and wearing silver wreaths
on their heads,
solemnly danced on bare feet
to the humming
of the poppies.
Under that orange, green, and purple melody,
the blind prophet fell
from his horse, and emptied all the
loneliness from his shoes.
It turned the snow as red as
sacrificial blood,
and the sparrows were purring
at the twin bears, who clawed
their way to the sky.
Leaping from star to star,
they spilled the clay bowls
and jars filled
with messianic water,
washing the doubts, muddy and red,
from the eyes of the sinners and the

mediocre followers. Clear-eyed,
they dressed themselves
in blue and green tunics, and joined
the dancing white-robed maidens,
painting with feet on the floor:
murals of the crumbling brown rituals
from yesterday, and
the quietly metallic anxiety
of tomorrow, and
the hope leaking
between our fingers today.

ARGUMENT IN THE CHAPEL

An unkindness of ravens
flutters above like ash,
mocking the suicidal snowflakes
breaking across windshields,
while a vagrant slams a screen door
in the temple's marble corridor,
rattling loose the upside-down handwriting
and the answers writhing away.
Card-carrying holy men, wearing
black coats and clandestine transactions
in the sanctuary,
burn piles of feathers—angel wings—
an offering sold
for black market promises.
And with my eyes burnt
by exhausted impatience,
I relent and run, heeding
some Cajun religion,
and inhabiting an unholy camp
with the adherents
of an unevolved culture.
I dance with those blasphemers
in the orange winter night,
dance under a marriage
of fire and sleet,

dance to lords of the underworld
with my bloody feet and
intoxicated hands upraised.
We renounce that pristine
and cultivated god,
apathetically enshrined under glass.
That god kicks mud and warheads
at the beggars, and laughs as they scrounge
for any glittery hope,
through filth and Third World alleys,
shivering and pathetically licking
at their pestilent fear.

The humble gardener never appears,
with grubby hands and overalls,
to help carry our patience,
weighty and awkward
like a ship or an engine.
And should such a mythical love-god exist,
could I ever show myself, raw
from the painted pagan dances?
With live blood spattering my clothes
and insolent spices knotting my hair?
Send me down with the exiles!
To linoleum rooms with
artificial air and light,

absorbing anything sanguine
from a thinking, anticipating body.
Yes! Send me down with the exiles,
and spare the innocents in my stead.

Black snow carefully smudges
a white-gray sky,
answering my hasty prayers.
And thus, I continue life
by a mercy undeserved.

SEARCHING FOR THE BIG SKIES

I told you last week
that someone planted
a plaster Virgin Mother
in a flower bed behind
some leafy red cabbage,
with a fiberglass reindeer shepherding the entire array.
And of all the dispersing pedestrians, not one
saw anything perverse or faulty, just continued blinking
into the sun spots, flipping the red and orange
radio frequencies in their heads.

But when you heard the Christmas geese
drifting past your window
on that hot green night at 2 a.m.,
you finally believed the truth:
the Ohio skies are shrinking.
And the starlings, like so many
copper petals and gongs,
heard that same sonic boom,
evacuating on hot feet and spicy wings
from the wicked flames invading their tall grass,
smoking like violated oil wells
and sad automobile tires.

Lost and wandering between the cookie cutters
in a steel and vinyl suburb,
you told me how you climbed a hill,
hoping that it might roll over, scratching
in its soporific adventures, and either gently or growling,
it might have offered you some direction.

But it wasn't even a real hill,
just a mound of construction site refugees,
a bed of roughhousing for backhoes and bulldogs.
Remember when we used to leave landscaping
to the migrating herds and the gods
of lava and tectonic cultivation?
Before we flew the banners of cartoon heroes
from our flag poles, and glued stickers of frogs
in the concrete next to the sanitary sewers?

You told me how
the rocks all started cracking and buzzing
because some chimaera had trapped
the black and yellow grasshoppers inside,
before they had the chance
to follow the starlings,
as the sky kept growing smaller and smaller.

AT THE GROCERY STORE

The priest spoke the truth. He grabbed my shoulders in the supermarket, canned corn in my hand. His eyes were those of a man chased, eyes like a rabbit, eyes like prey. And following, pushing the crowd, stalked a predatory man, with blackness pulled over his eyes, gnashing tiny, pointed teeth, swishing a hyena's tail behind him. The priest shook me and shouted, "Today is all you have!" And then he faded into glass, and fell, and broke on the tiled floor. Only afterwards did I notice his black and purple robes, while the clerks swept up his broken shards, lest the children cut themselves.

I did not buy the canned corn.
Instead, I stopped
while driving home,
to nestle into
the farmers' market.
The fresh cob in my hand
smelled of ivory goddesses
and very distant, very tall hills.

JUST ANOTHER WEDNESDAY

When I woke up Wednesday morning,
a flock of guitars was chasing my car,
wobbling on their stratospheric wings.
But still, there weren't any roses
being crushed beneath my tires,
only anarchists, crossing the road
sporadically, stealing mailbox flags
on their way to a broken river.
Those pilgrims wore sheepskin jackets and
executive suits, plumed hats with swords;
one small girl wore a pink hood
lined in white bear fur, and a young man
had wrapped himself
in his grandmother's quilt
cinched at the waist.
In bare or stockinged feet,
all toes popped against the shoreline snow
and the broken river coiled all their ankles.
They stood in the water,
                      watching a tiger.
She was hanging from an embankment
above the rolling exodus of glass and rocks,
clawing life by the inch
from that muddy shelf.

Her followers
          couldn't
                    help her.
They could only swallow light bulbs and candles,
wringing the luminescence from their pores
and their rhetorical tongues.

On another island, decorated
by a foreign ocean's feathers and medals,
an executioner asked his charge,
"Why do you only dance
of life and death, death and life?"
With a face like a sweeping kettle,
the prisoner answered,
"I cannot dance of love.
I haven't any yet."

THE NOMADS

Once every year, the nomads
file into my warehouse
with eyes of the hunted,
eyes of prey.
They're stapled to every last
bit of love they own,
and they come to barter
globes and crystal salt shakers
and faded names painted on
cinder blocks;
a market of objects, crowded
with the magic and love
of distance and travel.
These are the kings and dukes,
the noblefolk and the aristocrats,
who drop pinpricks and tear stains
across wood and strings and brass.
Sitting in circles, eating bread
and drinking exotic teas
brewed of scalding water and lilacs,
they whisper,
afraid of the eavesdropping echoes,
rocking their teacups
full of misconceptions.
They shake hands, exchange

incantations, cast prayers
like moths and arrows
across blended steel curls and black ribbons
and golden barbs.
Here there are no secrets,
no knowledge of plastics or circuitry;
just the ageless wonder at
fruit veins or insect wings, and the
alchemy one can access
with bare-soled feet
pressed into the dewy grass.

TERRESTRIAL NOSTALGIA

My friends are all gophers,
stashed secretly in earthy compartments.
The earth sighs and lives;
the very bedroom walls quiver and beat.
They shun the up-grounders and
the land of smoky hate,
sprinkles of holy water
guard their doorways from
ants and snakes and evangelists.

They build fires
in their tunnels and entryways.
And so they live,
eating earth-hearts inside earth-lights.
Sometimes, one little mole-friend owns
a small pantry, selling cream and rice
and paperclips.

And late in the darkness,
instead of sleeping,
they empty all the melodies
from their hand-spun guitars,
to carpet the footboards
and tack them to the walls.

While the trees, whose roots are
just passing through,
drink up stolen phrases,
and hum them to the nesting birds.

ACROSS THE RIVER

Ripples from a raven's tail,
fanning out like prayers and
cutting the sky from north to south,
washing the ambient
chatter from my head, wiping clean
the squared corners of thought.
No more spring-loaded trapdoors and
secret passages,
navigated with mirrors and crosses and
morphine; only a hot road unrolling ahead
and the potential for a white summer, alone.
But I can finally look across the river
filled with broken violins
and the burning chapters of greatness,
where a comet swims through the bedrock
and fish elope with eagles.
Hiding in the almond shade
of the opposite bank,
a wolf steals an old pair of my eyes,
re-colors the irises, and paces
the shoreline, treading a thick carpet
of muddy papers, the unfinished letters
and colored bills of misread conscience,
yet to be reconciled.
My sun-stained clothes

and well-traveled, heavy black shoes,
send fear spidering across her back.
But somehow, a strength holds
in her black feet and the white blazes
down her nose and cradling her eyes,
until flight takes her and I only see
how the holly and ivy underbrush
swallow the last flash of her tail.

I cannot follow, always trying
to elbow my way into someone else's fate.
I live on this side of the river now;
I walk among the tigers and I can finally call out
the names of the stars and the planets and moons.
But still, I think about the wolf,
praying for stone bridges and candles,
and lighting every darkened
corner of this alley.

INDIGO FREIGHT TRAIN

Listen to the howl of the June bug sock hop,
calling down the sparrows from their limousine stare.

Somewhere in the cemetery, bulldog freight trains
are crushing every adolescent ego in the way.

Purple ladies rocking in their back porch gasoline,
shooting at the kingfisher-perforated skies,

baking paper brownies in a supernova microwave,
sipping at their dragon's blood and kicking over kings.

Indigo! Indigo! Weeping for the bluesmen.
Indigo! Indigo! Melting paper dolls.

Knocking at the front door, lions on the telephone,
angels in the parlor chairs who wait to tell you lies,

duplicating underground wolf pack whirlpools,
and climbing up the black and yellow sunshine glass.

Maybe in the morning, under seagull stormbreak.
Maybe in the morning, after shedding mountain skins.

Maybe in the morning, when the bullfrog choir sings,

"Maybe in the morning,
maybe in the morning,"

Maybe in the morning, at the sanctuary door.

THROUGH MY ORANGE WINDOW

Even before I spotted
the white feathers
confettied across my back porch,
I saw the bloody handprints,
smeared across the sky.
Then I knew the dove was dead.
Lady Autumn stood by
guarding the scruffy carcass,
with her windy hair
and hollow bronze eyes,
smelling of wood smoke perfume and
gray, rippling puddles of memory,
of a generic childhood and the tainting
of wide-angle adolescence.
Dark loneliness birthed a second moon
on that gory night.
Between the dueling moons
circled a fog of ravens
carrying their alcohol and party hats
over an old and broken field.
Some weather god rattled
the spinning gold balls that measure time
and reached to part
the curtains of chaos in my eyes.
I squinted into the orange night,

searching for a pair of eyes
to hold my hand, and I found
a lost moth on paper wings
quietly bumping against the glass.

THROWING ROCKS

Breathless and dirty at my door,
he told me he'd barely escaped
the summer warriors
tornadoing through the garden,
slicing apart madness with machetes
and burning the flowers and
bloodying the hills. They ran
until they reached
the tree that he and I had
planted in the desert;
but with a knotted and rocky core,
they couldn't chop it down.

He told me about a power-mad lion
cradling the sun, and blasting holes
through the orange cliffs, trading
skins with the devil, and lighting
imploding fires on the lake beds,
failing as the water sang.
He told me about finding his own
secluded mountain, where
a solitary man could build or
destroy his own windfall,
his own snow and castles and lace.

But I know that he was just
pasting together cardboard palaces
from detergent boxes,
slapping his tie-dyed emotions
across the walls of telephone booths
and the doors of the bathroom stalls
in some kind of carnival barker's display
of mock bravery, flashing neon and
warped mirrors to hide a fear
of argyle cages and steel jaws reciting
the truth of choices, an exegesis
of transcendental chameleons.

He started to tell me
about magicians, working at their trade
hanging steel ships in the sky…
until I closed his mouth to stop the light:
I didn't want to see anymore shadows.

ALMONDS

Romeo discerned, with a
swampy eye,
"It's the nunnery for you, my dear!
No surgical alterations or
cupboards full of plastic knives!
Yea, it's the nunnery for you, m'dear!"

So I punched him in the front teeth.

"You soggy excuse for a
used teabag!"
I retorted, with salt rocks and chlorine.
"You couldn't hear hyenas
gnawing at your boxer shorts!
Or notice the black flies
camping out in your nostrils,
building tiny bon-fires, roasting marshmallows!
Can't you smell the marshmallows?!

"Hopeless? *Hopeless!?*
There's some news from the cookie jar, Mister
five-to-nine, solitaire online
remote potato salad
tongs, with a twist of 'hey, that's
my change!' and a
swollen fourth toe!

"Why don't you just
run that sugary little tuxedo
through the riding mower
before I loose the coffee grounds and
parakeets to
have their way with your
polyester-shiny oxfords
on your way down
the alfalfa chute?!"

LAMENT AND CHRONICLE

Some clotted old scholars
in choking plaid bow-ties
garbled and cobbled
my words into bowls and plates of a
more serious shade: black. A cast iron.
Words by their filter
must precariously drip of
sex God myth angst love death poverty war—and—
violence. Carefully measured rules forbid
the errant poeticization of a word like

donuts.
Donuts. Or
stock car racing. Or just the word
"quack". As in ducks.

They, the infamous, do not like
donuts, and the clutter thereby entailed.
Thus shall I stage forthwith
a donut revolution, the
glorifying of fried batter and
sticky glaze. My comrades and I
shall sit on the floor at a low table,
playing chess, for,
ours is a

sophisticated revolution with
crullers for pawns, the king as
a fat jelly, and the game
must be called on account of
a gruesome custard skirmish.
Then, we'll all run into the night,
painted and chanting and singing
the fight song of baked goods.

Before we all fall into a pond.

Quack!

Tomorrow, I will try
some stock car racing.

PARANOIA

I woke up humming a country song
that I've never heard before. And I don't like
that twangy stuff.
But before I opened my eyes, I saw fields
of curlews, hibernating for winter,
and horses whose hooves
cut the sky,
bleeding the red-black sun,
and striping the trees.

When I opened my eyes,
my gray cat was perched on the headboard
wondering his selfish cat-wonderings
about whether I know his god
who licks him warm and clean
in the yellow window.
He wonders if I think and dream and
hear the shrieking moths in the closet and
the mice serenading
at their mouse formal balls
under the floor.
No. He is bored.

He does not ask me. Instead he says his
morning prayers, stretching on my pillow,
with curled tongue and a would-be roar,
if he were a tiger, which
he is not. Nor is he even a cat.

Because I do not own a cat.

So I must still be dreaming, even
as I write this, laboring like the
songsmith, meticulously curling
one small note around the next,
watching the chain string out
from his mouth. This poem
is not a poem, but mental leftovers
from last night's television
and scented candles.
Maybe once I wake, I'll remember
this country song's three chords,
bitter tasting, because the theme is
always retread.

RAIN

No Renaissance man
painting glittery wings
ever really saw an angel.
Because I know that
the hems of angel robes
are always damp and muddy.
Didn't those famous luminaries
know how the choirs and guards
and seraphim
stood barefoot along the sidewalks,
blaring their herald trumpets
when a plague of frogs
in a thunderstorm—
that river of sprinkled and hopping green—
came rolling and chirruping
down the street,
announcing God's arrival?

How can anyone not love the Weather?
Its tunnels of sound and water
echo the oldness
as far back as Old can go.
Weather travels, wandering, visiting
every continent and ocean.

But mostly it licks—your face,
your hair, your mind,
your heart—clean,
tough and strong,
with a mamma tiger's love-tongue.

THE RABBITS OF ST. JOSEPH

We used to be young,
in basements and parlors
and bedrooms.
But now, we are gray,
and in the kitchen, under
the dusty, cricketing lights,
my thumb slowly stroking
the finish from my coffee cup.
You've poured my grandmother's jar
of starfish and beach glass
on the table between us.
Each rounded trapezoid and bead
wraps around
an oblique memory,
frozen as in amber.
You and I finger them,
our hands hot from the past and
the talk and the coffee,
melting the glass.
And the little petrified squares,
stolen from the minds
of friends and strangers,
flap their wings and leave
through the open window,

butterflies and white doves
and silver bats that stick to the sky,
building new constellations,
arching over the day when

black lions broke down doors,
demanding a father too young and
a small girl too old,
like some sepia-toned drama.
You and I were only children then, draping
sharp battle robes across
t-shirts and jeans, fighting with
sticks and swords and
arrows and dynamite,
while fear crawled
through the keyholes,
through our ears.
And we ran,

excavating prayers from beneath
wooden pianos, and unearthing
a shaky old cigar box
filled with sleeping souls.
Once awakened,
they sold us a train ticket
bound for the edge of the world.
The steel heart beat through our feet
and our minds, bending consciousness

into sculpted metal corners, until
we stepped off, tumbling
into St. Joseph's grass, a garden
of overlapping mirrors and toppled crosses.
The yard had grown thickly with
statues and old elfin magic, guarded
by the beatified rabbits
who swam rivers and climbed temples,
who flew, and disappeared.
Beneath those one hundred pairs of brown eyes,
you wrote your hopes
across my face, the felt pen
tickling the bridge of my nose,
before we ran into the sea: two gulls
destined for immortality,
pushing through enchanted oil curtains
into second space.

RUN, RUN 'TIL YOU'RE FAR AWAY

The tiger runs
with brass in her claws
and bells on her tail
and steam in her lungs.

The tiger runs
with sparks threatening her fur,
and her eyes broken into stones,
and the street scalding her feet.

The tiger runs,
dodging as the ceilings drip
into her path.
She tangos the racecourse
between trees,
and people,
and people turned
into trees

in the wood of the suicides,
bordered by the shrubs
of those who never bothered
to scrape their knees
and peer over locked gates,
indulging their forbidden faces.

They cuddle their engraved clocks
and their reclining chairs and
their sliding rulers, hiding under
black hats and
never learning to cry.

The rabbit runs,
dressed in silver necklaces and bracelets,
kicking the moon and
the asteroid's belt.
And she outpaces the boatman,
and the boatman's dog,
and every murky lake and river
flowing loosely
with jealous and watery hands.

BETWEEN

Muslim poets chant
in spinning meditations
around marble pillars
supporting the mosque.

They speak broad and
sweeping rugs, oriental patterns
with spiced designs.
Brushstrokes from their mouths,

now fall green on canvas
and fabric—but an independent
green, not the green neighboring
blue and yellow.

And only between this green's
hallowed walls, feathered and furred,
origins unknown, only here
do you step through to

embrace.

STORY

I have a friend
who paints
grandiose equine landscapes
on the backs of old tea bags,
persistently scented with
black and green,
blueberry and chamomile.
He constructed seaweed and
hoboes and toothpick collages.

And she
followed him,
with paper bags,
collecting the ashen,
glittery nightness
shaken from his hair
and shoes.

They were in love.

And on the road, though
riding on a glory-blue Ferris wheel,
chasing the police and
wading through
public school swamps and

corporate playgrounds,
past a trailer filled with platinum cars,
claiming the ground
under a purple tent;
the stuff of novels and Americana,
clean pages, crisp fonts,
plenty of smiling, color photos.

She
almost died,
a red line, writing names in the dark,
embracing an antique
copper lamp, shaped
like the woman at the well.

So, he
braced himself in the frame,
trying to stretch the window.
"It isn't big enough," he said.
"The sunlight will never fit,"
he said.
"The autumn green,"
he said,
"would be nicked and chipped,
trying to fit through
that little pane."
With elbows and knees at the corners,
he's trying to stretch the window.

TRIPPING OVER GIANTS

When the bobcats wail
and the bloodhounds bay
so inharmoniously that the leaves turn red,

then, a woman,
with a face like a tree
and a yet unnamed color to her skin,
walks the streets.
She wears green in her hair
and gold in her ears
and gold on her wrists,
around her neck, her waist,
her toes,
gold in her eyebrows and
trickling, gingerly,
across her lashes.
And the children stop; they
drop their hot dogs and
baseballs and pieces of chalk,
release their final grasp
on that last heat, the last splinters of sun,

and they follow her into the woods, to
live in pewter cherry trees and
learn to sing in a language
of copper and bronze and
run with teams of sled dogs over glaciers.

Then, the regal bear
wrapped around an apple tree,
crowned with silver and rubies,
claws of steel and granite,
climbs down to my bedside
while I sleep, and whispers,

light as suede and dark as glass,

that I must go walking
with pearls in my shoes,
tripping over giants and bumping my forehead
while passing under bridges.
And there,

there, croons the bear in my ear,
I'll meet a certain man.
And never before have I met such a man
with fate so readily seeping
into his footsteps.

ON THE DAY OF BROKEN BELLS

A window separates
my room and yours,
where the crippled doves
beat against the glass,
mute and frustrated, lacking
teeth or fuel.
We long to shed our skins,
mix and exchange, becoming
patchwork-quilted cousins,
taste-testing the bits of
neighboring passion and talent.
Instead, pipe smoke and
fancy script mock
all human emotion, constructing
papier-mâché palaces
in the rain.
We can hear the wingéd cats,
swarming outside; a massacre of
the bluebirds, those delicate berries,
jewels strung through
the willow's branches.
Only the bitters extracted

from eucalyptus boughs
remain, as we attempt to
reassemble the
little, broken felt pieces,
attempting the reordering of atoms.

UNCERTAINTY

I think we've stretched
the blackened windows
too tight
across our catacomb walls,
taped and patched at the seams.
The screaming city
still finds us down here,
boring through the rock and the
sheets of industrial noise.
The walls crack under pressure
and crystal ashes rain from the
black ceiling tiles,
dampening any fluffy hearts
beating under the neon-lighted politics
and too many flags
draped across the rafters.
Weasels and ferrets
burrow through the loose mortar,
spilling fur underfoot, wrapping around
the wooden legs of tables and chairs.
And behind the door of a locked back room,
someone is burning
all the old papers
and photos and records.

We will all barely escape
from this cave tonight,
squinting through the pink and black smoke
that hangs from our brows.
The ivory strings of lonely dead men
thread through the floor boards,
channeled by dancers with
feathers on the soles of their shoes.
They used to decorate the sand
around archaic bonfires
with their fancy footprints,
conjuring doves and singing blackbirds.
Now those feathers barely rattle
against the corners of the ceiling,
while a defrocked piano virtuoso
tries to prop up the pressured roof
by stacking many-tiered chords,
one on top of the next.

RELUCTANT HALLELUJAH

How many black cars
parked in the beaded rain tonight?
How many men in dark, woolen suits,
line the walk, leaning and watching,
while children crawl
through the dirt and leaves and shifting rocks?

You and I—we used to pretend
with paint and wood and screens
in front of the back-lit legends,
while the street lamps outside my house
flickered in the shimmering, flying hate.

Now, I can't even find
the tiny blue lights
tattooed beneath your eyes
one hundred years ago,
when the lonely pilgrims, on their knees,
reached for names
in granite and green marble.

But you refuse to pluck your name,
retreating from my mouth,
and you refuse to throw out my petitions,
washing in the salty river.
Because, still and quiet, a feathered,
black-and-gold memory comes,
barely chirping, barely seen,
but mending the pink blaze of hope
hidden inside of every worry,
unreachable by doctors or politicians.
And encircled by the humming,
gray shells of ancestors,
I joined their belated chanting,
singing up, through knotted lightening,
of hallelujah.

EXIT

A left-handed star
fell, still hot,
into the unburned sidewalk,
to be scavenged and chewed
by an untrained clutch of gryphon,
dripping scrutiny and harsh smoke
down the necks of impetuous travelers.
So I picked up the star, pitted and
gnawed, but still silver,
until I lost myself,
cutting through
a maze of unlit candles.
Incandescent lamps were falling
through the hole in my jacket pocket,
smashing the medicine for
the relief of fear.
Deceptive arrows haunted the footlights,
blocking any view of a
glowing exit,
and glass violins poured
over the sunburned patterns in my skin,
cooling the surface tension.
Until two men with soft gray wings
landed in my path, with uncut feet.
They scraped the mud and smog

from behind my ears,
and pressed ashes into blue gold,
forging ladders and skyscrapers.
They offered me
a goldsmith apprenticeship,
but in a maze without doors,
I protested that I couldn't leave,
couldn't close the chapter
with a bear hiding between the pages.
One opened my fist, finally
releasing the star, before they
wrapped me in a hammock
of feathers and cotton,
showing me how
to fall from windows
and walk along the rooftops.

DEUS EX MACHINA

Wolf prints shuffle around a metal carousel,
climbing the constellations, and snaking
trellises of light around the
dragon wheels and Grecian columns.
Fireflies crouch in the catwalks,
chasing the gilded archers and
major league kings from
beneath these vaulted ceilings.

And up ahead, liars or prophets or
footlight phantoms;
they're rhapsodizing,
guitars opened wide into
battle ships and banquet halls,
casting red and yellow faces, flickers
against a storm-blue backdrop,
lit by the scars of meteor claws.

In the wings, the boxes, the raccoons hum
while the katydids dance a
slow, slow, tango.
And behind the curtains and
the symphonic valves, the Sunday organists are
shuttling drum kits and
the last few glitters of a leftover
Johnny Cash tune.

From the front row, we
clutch our orange
construction tickets,
living with our arms in the air,
and bartering
for a little extra twilight,
watching, as two falling stars collide,
forging molten orbits forever.
And we read answers in the
descent of salty calligraphy and
the spoonfuls of rain,
tracing circles in the lake.

Blue and cool,
cupped in the palm of my hand,
the world, tonight, is very tiny,
and mostly, full of light.

THE NIGHT CHILDREN

When my cheek meets the pillow,
they step from the closet
and the dressers and the air conditioner,
wearing rosaries of tiny bells
around their necks and ankles.
Daemons or faeries
or some other avatars
built of dust and clay,
they are the heathen nymphs
who wrote King David's psalms, and
the scruffy angels who sang
the Eddas to the Vikings.
Now under the same darkness,
they clack around my bed
wearing my high heels against
the hardwood floors,
rifling through my thesaurus and Bible,
slapping their muddy handprints
against the soffit and
my nocturnal dreams.
Together we could play hide-and-go-seek,
or gnaw on the chess pieces
because we've forgotten
the rules of black and white,
of queens and horses, serfs and groveling bishops.

Playing with the night children,
we might grow wings of a hybrid aviation,
of feathers, and scales, and fur:
Man's evolution into an iridescent race of familiars,
singing with the cave painters
who saved their prayers forever,
glittering inside the rocks.

But tonight, there are no visitors; I can't find those
booming iconic myths
that the child always craved.
No golden eagles, no winged goddesses
skating to earth on the blizzard clouds.
And the best story that I can tell
to the row of candles lining my windowsill
is about the profile on the back of a dime,
and how it laughs in the air as we gamble.

A PEDESTRIAN UNEXPECTED

A small, cute Japanese lady
in lavender and green
stopped me on the street today.
Her eyes flashed like a gypsy's
and her fingers wore a fortune teller's rings,
but she smiled enough foreign camaraderie
to snag me in a pause,
listening to the snuggling warmth
of her halting English; accidental accents and
chopped suffixes. No matter.
No matter.
With my chin between her thumb and finger
she sweetly declared
that my face belonged to
Joan of Arc in a recent movie.
"Look it up," she said.
And she dictated to me that my hair,
worn down, and long, was
"charming."
Then she evaporated, floated away
on the mid-day tide pools of people
swirling through the city sidewalks.

I pinched my arm running home,
expecting a paralyzing tornado
or a volcano's lava river
or a rain of small pale demons
with fangs and yellow eyes:
the usual inhabitants of nightmares.
But none of the dead met and spoke to me
of the impossible as paper-dry
matter-of-fact,
and I thus divined that I was awake.

So I folded up the Japanese woman,
a memoried scent of
magic and tea and confidence,
and hid her in my sock drawer.
Maybe tomorrow, she
won't be there.
Or maybe, just maybe,
she will.

3 A.M. IN HOTEL KAZAKHSTAN

Scratching the fleas
from my hair, this afternoon
I discovered a small hole
in the back of my head.
It must be where the madness
leaks in.
Oh, don't worry.
Not *that* kind of madness.
Only the celestial kind,
with delusions of
epic importance;
the prophetic breed of madness,
smacking cowbells
and wearing potato sacks and lampshades,
because divine wisdom's creativity
heeds no social norms.
Yea, I say, it sets them.
Yes, the celestial kind of madness,
which revealed to me
the barefooted giants
in hoodies and track pants.
(Why do people always insist
that giants dress in the garb of
four or five centuries ago, give
or take? Why couldn't giants

maintain an updated wardrobe?)
But they are always barefoot.
It is very hard to find shoes
that large. Or even
nice dress boots
with heels.
But the giants try
to fool us, hanging up
their sequined curtains
and hoping we believe
in stars. Oh?
Did they fool you too?
A common mistake, really.
But actually, the stars
have all poured down
the bathtub drain,
which is why the sewers back
into the streets, and we
find ourselves with a slop
of candle wicks and painted glass,
across which our camels
must tiptoe.
Fortunately, they've all been
classically trained in ballet,
with their toenails painted fuchsia,
and mauve or sea foam green
highlights in their hair.
I also found a wood nymph

in my ear today. He had dreadfully
curled little horns and
played a wooden flute
with his nostrils. The
louse-ridden vermin
almost convinced me,
with his sneaky whisperings,
that the moon is round and
not square at all.
Fortunately, I plucked him out
while I was rooting around
for a breakfast of sanity.
Have you seen it?
It looks like steel
ball-bearings, and rattles
like peanuts in the kitchen sink.

SAVING SOULS

I first took
my office mate for a wood nymph
because she left behind a scent—not evil but
still enigmatically forbidden—
whenever she left a room.
A tree, a ginko, growing from my desk
when I arrived at work today,
confirmed my suspicions.
So I stood, instead of sitting,
birthing illegitimate children
and bundling them in bushels,
ears of corn,
shipping them to Iowa.
She
laughed, cupping handfuls of holidays
into her ears and pockets
to snack on later, with almonds
or walnuts.
Hate songs hung from the tree,
but we folded them into pigeons,
blowing them out the windows with
tiny messages reading "save our souls"
tied to their legs.
Unfortunately, eyes bulging from the walls
intercepted any foreign-bound saviors:

Executives do love stewing tiny messiahs
in the lunchrooms,
garnished with chives and parsley,
although the feathers stick between their teeth.
So, maybe tomorrow, we will plant a crop of
soy beans in the hallways and
bring along the harvest goddess to help.

THE BABIES OF THE STONE WINGS:
THE FINAL SONG OF MILO

Milo the Prophet
woke on the morning
when the trees exploded a
violent purple
across the sidewalks,
for joggers and walking dogs
to crush the broken pieces.
He brushed the seven dwarves
and a small flock of wood gnomes
from his still sleepy hair,
and announced to us
that the world was ending,
very soon.
And so he could (and would)
hike the Atlantic to New Zealand
by way of Africa, he said,
(because he had never seen
the Lion)
because one can only hike an ocean
when the world is ending.
He would be leaving
that afternoon, from a Carolina beach,
and we, the Disciples of Milo,
all fire and ducks,

went to toss farewells and our eyes
at his back,
while he walked to Africa.
And out came the nuns,
full-habited in penguin glory,
from their catacombed seclusion.
They danced Irish jigs in the street;
even the Ukrainian nuns
who were not Irish,
because they knew
that Milo was right,
and that the world was ending,
very soon.
It stormed that day.
The Sky came down, panting
July steam at the long, brown Street.
And the nuns just kept dancing.
I stopped, removing
my soggy gray socks
and tennis shoes, wet
in the end-of-the-world storm,
to let my naked toes squoosh and wallow
in the clear, sweet mud of insanity.
Babies leapt from strollers,
and toddlers, sprinting from their mothers' hands,
stole the stone wings from
cemetery angels and flew,
North, to Aurora's borealis.

And a black-and-gold giant
left his deep footprints,
mercury ponds,
through my neighbors' backyards,
while he picked stars and the moon,
dangling cherries in the night, to eat.
And then it was dark.
Only the owls were
hoo-hoo-ing their sound effects
under green X-trails of planes.
So I ran to the water tower
and climbed that pencil-thin ladder,
because heights don't matter
when it is dark and the world is ending,
very soon.
And the Spanish lady professors below
were chasing moths with nets,
waiting for the thumb of God.
At the top, the wind
of dancing party gowns
billowed in my shirt, a parachute
to catch the Babies of the
Stone Wings,
because their mothers had
no faith
in flight, thinking
they would fall.
But they didn't.

The air smelt of feet
running someplace destined,
and I looked toward Africa,
for, maybe, a bobbing speck
that was Milo.
That water tower was so high
that the sky wrapped
layers of blue scarves right around me,
and I remembered
that Milo once told me
how some souls velcro together
at meeting,
and others only slip,
greased and friction-less.
And alone up there,
breathing the narrow air
in my blue sky-cocoon,
I waited.

NOTE FROM THE ANONYMOUS LOVER

Follow the salt trails and
orchid-scented handprints
to a corrugated meadow,
a blanket over mines of bread
and temptation.
Here, robins nest in hope
and ducks will scatter diamonds
across the lake,
hollering glories toward
muddy, unshaped children.
Anxiety claws at the concrete;
leave it behind with the
pebbles and trash!
You must run into this land
of silver halos and dusky blue
swallows tented in the pines.
Flashlights walk toward
the eastern falls, overflowing with
boxes of light, and
the sweetest illusions breed fire
in your feet.

Love,
        bare your green wings
now, and cut them
against the purple thunder,
that you might read your fate
penned above your head
by strange monks peddling
mysticism and neon signs.

LOCKING WINDOWS, LIFTING CEILINGS

I've got nothing left to live on;
no food, no water,
just this stale night air
and one more road sign
losing a fight with my taillights.

And I'm never going back to sleep,
afraid that I'll start seeing faces.
Faces under book covers
and wrapped in violin strings
and painted
into the walls
where they watch me while I dress.

I'm just smiling through the person
I'll never be:
the girl who doesn't need a man,
and never worries that she
might have been looking
the wrong way,
on the morning when fate
ran by.
The girl sitting proudly in the corner,
who never notices her empty hand,
who throws rocks in the river

and her arms in the sky
and her shoes in the street, just
so her feet
can laugh with the grass.

The girl who smiles on rainy mornings
and never looks over her shoulder,
because she knows that she's right,
that the Buddha and the tarot
and the canonized saints
are all pushing on her elbows
with the help of the sunshine.

Do I look like her? Power suits
and business heels and
perfect, perfect eye make-up?
Sassy hips and boyish hair, and
never looking twice? Only
ever living for herself.

I'm not her.

I have to braid my own gold rings
and dig my own boxes of diamonds;
crack my own cloudy window panes
and smash my own plates,
                      for no reason.

Until there's nothing left for me to live on;
Just the empty blood of this old night air,
and one more mile, broken
under my tires.

SAILOR

A tern weaves,
navigating the waves of air
over the marsh grass.
Her milk-smooth wings
trim the sky's uneven edges
to fall in locks and float on the water.
The wind, teased into the chase
but baffled by the threads of her dance,
trips and ties himself in knots.
She balances above me,
a marionette suspended
yet conducting the strings,
and she rides, like a stroking bow
coaxing sweet chords.
He holds her motionless,
her orange-red splinter of a beak,
poised to strike me, the intruder in her marsh,
but with a twist of ribbon wings
the wind responds,
and bears her over the river.

ESCAPE TONES

I lay pressed beneath a wooden ceiling
pocked with one-thousand eyes
and housing hooded dozens
who pass chipped and shell-thin ceramic
back and forth. And muttering,
always muttering, between the lilacs.
From behind the side wall, I could hear
a scraping; metal noises, the iron and tools
of loose and broken things
that might burn the roof of my mouth.

I ran outside and started building bells
from the things that didn't matter anymore,
hammered from small injuries
and discarded wallpaper
used for hiding the smoky ghost veins
crackling in the paint and dry wall.

Someone wrote all the road signs in crayon
and melted them in the rain of
lost shoes and buttons falling from grace,
bruising the travelers' shoulders and songs,
which they try to hide beneath newspapers,
printed with yellow ribbons and helicopters.

I hung the bells from trees and stray door lintels
to chase away the cave monsters—
the sea minks and the rabbit women—
and just to see if the birds would notice
the parade chimes, the jeweled and inset chimes,
the tarnished uncertain chimes, or
the reconditioned faith chimes.
And if the ceiling fell again,
would the cuckoo bird continue singing
his funereal songs of deception?

Once again empty-handed
beneath a widely suspicious evening,
I spotted your silhouette up the street,
pouring a bowl of cricket songs
over your bruised and broken fingers.
I ran toward you, hoping it could also cure
my lonely feet and fallen arches.

DETOUR

Don't you swallow those thickened words,
choking in your throat
like a ball of old lace.
Not now. Not when birdsong and water
flow through the radiator pipes,
and the dogwood blossoms
rain sonatas, melting the walls
off the cardboard minimall,
while the beaded lampshades
leak purple and orange
to wrestle with your fingertips
in an iron bowl of black lava sand.

People don't know.
They unleash
their golden dogs to climb through the orchards,
and they forget about record players
left on the lawn.
They're too busy stuffing their minds
in plastic bags and their hearts
between the coils of motorcycle engines
to even notice the ball of lightening,

trapped and rolling in the neighbor's backyard,
or the net of 26,000 lights
draping the hill under an empty sky:
The sky that we emptied.

And now we look up, wondering why
we can't see the stars,
when we
pulled them all to the ground,
knotting up all the traffic signals,
sending the sheep to the desert
and the camels to the springs.

Sometimes you just take a wrong turn
and you still have to keep going,
rocking on a sailboat
between November thunder,
and skating into glacier-clean sunshine.

LOST

No windmills here in this town:
only bridges, with wine flowing beneath
and soldiers walking above,
wearing darkened, stony eyes
that reach over railings and into mirrors
and the smeared reflections
paved into the wet night streets.

And we are all those soldiers

fighting the bullet holes through the curtains,
barricading the doors with furniture against
the men without ears or faces,
who swing clubs, breaking our walls, trying to steal
the scarves from our necks
and the legends from our minds.
Thieves and intervening monsters,
with their twisted blackened fingers,
left us wrapped in barbed wire
among the garden of half-eaten roses.

Blue suits imposed on a green field
watch the last of the flowers dissolve,
next to the scholars frantically leafing
through their holy books.

But the children know the answers
to mending the injured psyches, the crippled lives;
just by pointing small fingers toward
the silver in the sky,
they pass unharmed between
the slats in the fences.

And so we leave, driving around
the north side of the mountain,
carried by starlings and ravens
into the west end of paradise.

OUT OF THE DESERT

A liar and a cheater,
like a crayon-painted road sign
melting waxy puddles through
tomorrow afternoon, I
never quite believed
in men with wings—
big and great golden eagle wings,
growing from their shoulder blades—
no. I never quite believed,
although I said I did.

Because I always watched my brothers,
carrying the weather on their backs,
past the blue welding light,
scouring the steam-loving cranes
until they burned and bled and
cracked all the gunmetal nightlights,
lifting iron ladders, girders
crossed into star-shaped flowers
worshipping a dead and contrived
second sun.

And I said no.

I painted neon pink and silver
over all the attic drywall,
called it Heaven, climbed those eighteen stairs
every afternoon at four o'clock,
said my prayers, almost
thought I heard the saints
talking back to me.

And then I stood on the crystal jukebox
declaring, in forty different tongues
like a knighted prophet in
leather sandals and a corduroy tunic, that
yes, I believe
men can grow
glossy wings from their backs,
crossing canyons and vaulting the rapids.

I had to believe.
But I never quite believed.

And the doubt? I knew it,
a chewing nest of carpenter vermin
drinking the ink out of prayer books
and clipping black eyes to the curtains.

They chased me from the cathedral,
from the railroad, from the statehouse.
They chased me from the school and
from the grocery, from the park.

They chased me to an old garage
underneath an old factory.
And there, without fish-tail testimonials
or a porcelain-faced audience,
there, I found
a man, with wings,
who showed me how
to find my own, auburn and burgundy-feathered,

crossing lakes and vaulting
the heroic moon I'd never met.
And finally, finally, I believed.